Howard Blake

Walking in the Air

arranged for Piano Quartet
(2014)

Score and set of parts

Chester Music

'WALKING IN THE AIR'

for violin, viola, cello & piano
specially arranged for Gloucester Music Society, Christmas 2014

HOWARD BLAKE
op.661 November 30th 2014

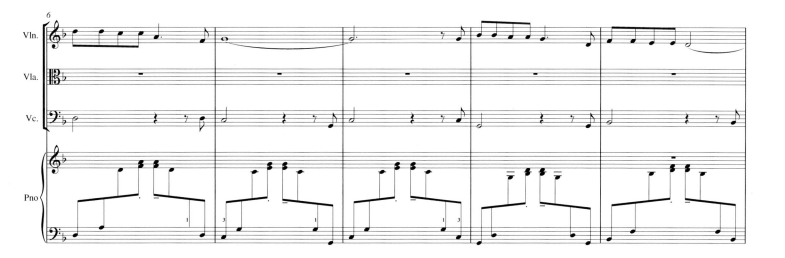

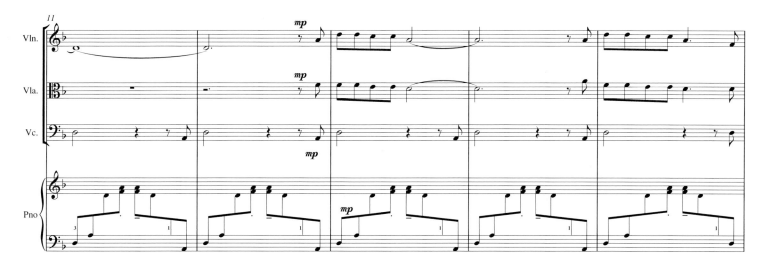

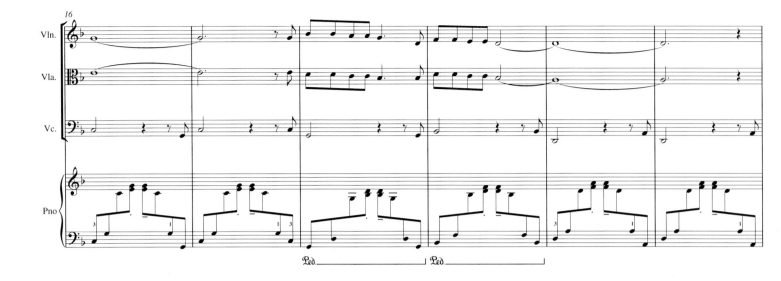

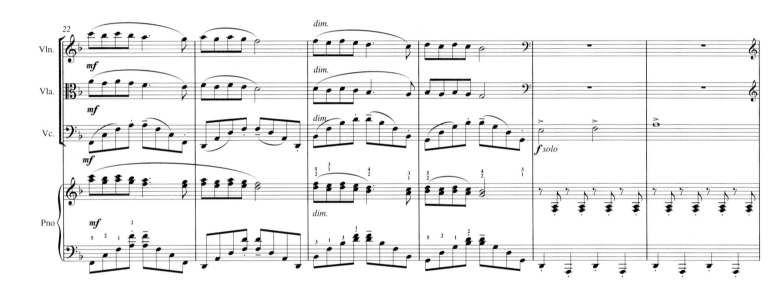

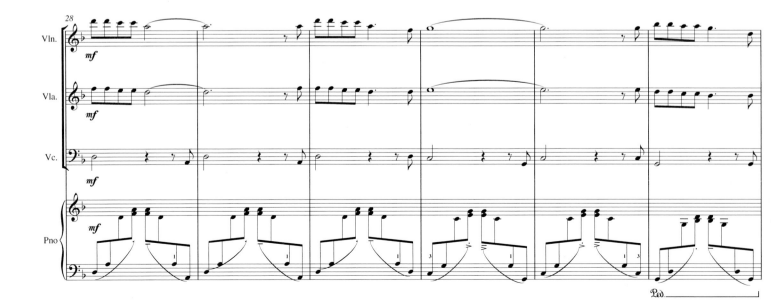

Howard Blake

Walking in the Air

arranged for Piano Quartet
(2014)

Violin part

Chester Music

2

Violin

'WALKING IN THE AIR'

for violin, viola, cello & piano
specially arranged for Gloucester Music Society, Christmas 2014

HOWARD BLAKE
op.661 November 30th 2014

Violin

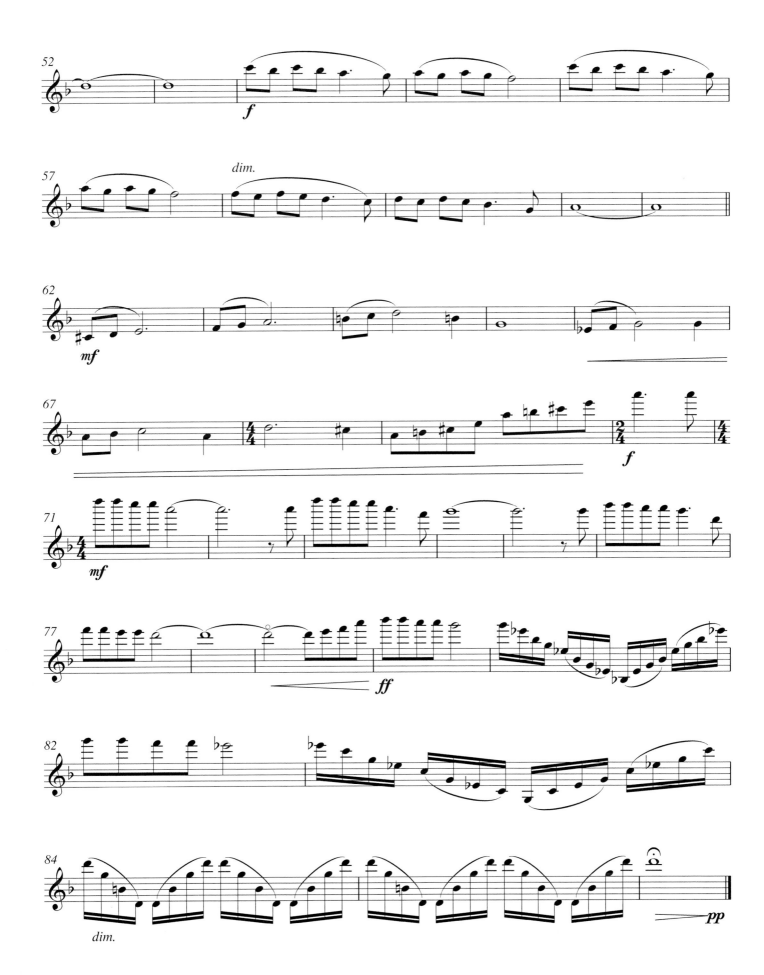

Howard Blake

Walking in the Air

arranged for Piano Quartet
(2014)

Viola part

Chester Music

'WALKING IN THE AIR'

for violin, viola, cello & piano
specially arranged for Gloucester Music Society, Christmas 2014

HOWARD BLAKE
op.661 November 30th 2014

Viola

Howard Blake

Walking in the Air

arranged for Piano Quartet
(2014)

Violoncello part

Chester Music

2
Violoncello

'WALKING IN THE AIR'

for violin, viola, cello & piano
specially arranged for Gloucester Music Society, Christmas 2014

HOWARD BLAKE
op.661 November 30th 2014

Moderato

Violoncello

3

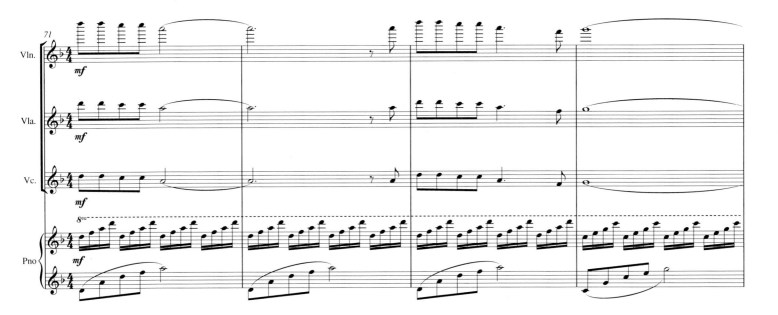

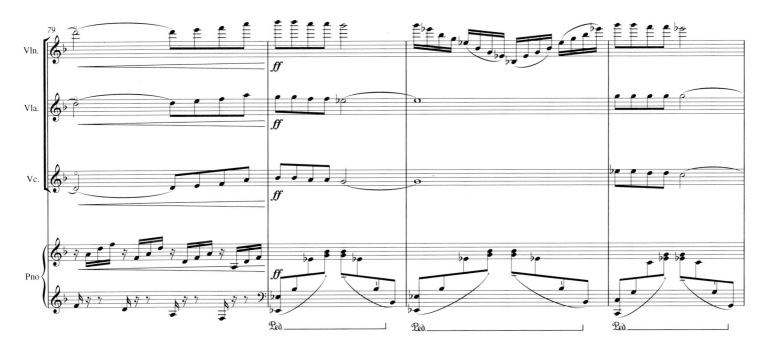

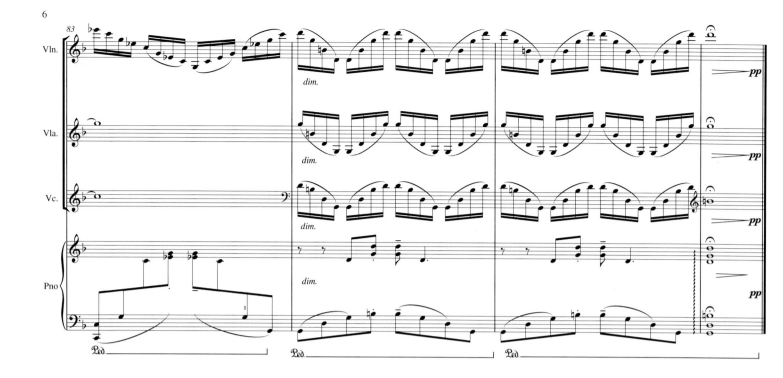